Who Is

G. C. Jones

Volume 1

By

G.C. Jones

TABLE OF CONTENTS

INTRODUCTION

I am Gerald C. Jones, #M9993231 in the book titled 'The Isaac Mize Family of Eastern Kentucky' (Miller Jr., 1985). I have always been interested in genealogy, and my desire for knowledge increased greatly recently when I had a chance to re-read the book on one branch of my family called 'The Isaac Mize Family of Eastern Kentucky' (Miller Jr., 1985).

Through-out my entire life, people have always asked me 'who is G. C. Jones?' Sometimes they ask me directly 'who are you', but most of the time they wait until I have left and ask others 'who was that?' So, it made me ask myself, who am I really? Am I a nobody, or am I from a long line of somebody's? When I thought about it, I knew deep within myself that the later was true.

Since I found too much information to soak in that fast, I decided to write it all down for future reference. This is my family lineage through my mother's side of my family. Further volumes will be including my father's lineage, lineage of others related to me, and more importantly volumes explaining why you probably already knew of G. C. Jones.

It was at this time that I decided to create a small project that showed my direct lineage from Isaac Mize to me through my mother's side of my family. I do thoroughly enjoy reading about all branches of the Isaac Mize family and hope at some point in the future to meet each and every one of them in person. My project has led me to the collection of writings that you are currently about to enjoy.

It is my hope and intentions that any person in the Isaac Mize family would be able to take the process that I used to create this list of people for my direct lineage, and use it in their own branch of their own family to show their own direct lineage from our ancestors to the lives we are living today. In my opinion, it will make the relationship between us and our ancestors feel more personal.

I hope everyone enjoys this collection of stories and facts about this branch of the Isaac Mize family, and I also hope it will educate and inspire future generations to feel as encouraged to learn about their family as it has done for me.

I have found in my research what I believe to be information that dates the Mize family back to around 1595 in Lancashire England. It is a marriage document for Thomas Mize from the Church of Latter-Day saints. It is not proof that he is in our family tree, but it is the only link I have found to this date. There are other documents that I have found that may add more details to some facts that are shown to us in the works of Franklin Miller Jr. when he wrote what I consider to be the best research book to ever delve into our family tree, entitled 'The Isaac Mize Family of Eastern Kentucky'.

Please enjoy this small humble collection of information and feel free to contact me if you see any details that are wrong, or have any information to add to this collection.

G.C. Jones

MIZE COAT OF ARMS

"At least four quite different MIZE coats of arms have been described. In the opinion of the author, these are harmless flights of fancy, but there is not one shred of evidence that they apply to our family. I take a dim view of coats of arms for several reasons.

1.) We cannot trace our MIZE family to an ancestor on the other side of the Atlantic whose name and place of residence are known. Only for such a name would a coat of arms have significance for a living descendant of the family which is the subject of this book.

2.) Our 17th century ancestors are really quite remote; the lines spread out fantastically. For example, all Mize descendants in this book are, we believe, descended from James Mize who was tithed in Virginia in 1694. But let's face it: for a typical adult family member such as M5154321, James

Mize was one of 512 male ancestors of the same generation. Any Mize coat of arms, even if correct, would represent only a small fraction of this person's ancestry. How about the other 511 family names?

3.) There is a good possibility — even a probability — that many of our immigrant ancestors who came to America in the 17th century were poor, had to struggle to get here, and left behind no family connections among the class of people who had lands and coats of arms. A coat of arms is, of course, an incentive to study and preserve one's heritage. Coats of arms are decorative and serve as conversation pieces. But for our own Mize family, they have no proven significance" (Miller Jr., 1985).

However, I would like to add a note on a coat of arms. If one has what they consider to be a coat of arms, then it can be beneficial to the individual. It can inspire and motivate their soul to search for more answers about their own family history. So even if the coat of arms is accurate or not, it may not matter to the true inspiration that one's own soul can possess by having a coat of arms to represent their branch of the family.

Let us also not forget that if we start off with what we believe to be our coat of arms, then the inspiration that we receive from that coat of arms could be what drives us to research further, and further, until we find the answers, and possibly the true coat of arms that we need to properly represent our own branch of the family.

In the Beginning

"In 1786 ISAAC MIZE was a young farmer in Surry County in the Yadkin Valley of northwestern North Carolina. Many of his relatives had come from the Southside of Virginia a generation earlier. Isaac had a strong desire to go west. With his wife Elizabeth and five children he moved to the frontier across the mountains and settled in Kentucky County of Virginia in newly-established Madison County. Here the Kentucky River emerges from its headwaters in the Blue Ridge Mountains and enters the eastern part of the attractive and fertile Bluegrass Region of Kentucky.

Isaac Mize spent the remaining 33 years of his life in the part of Madison County that became Estill County a year before he died in 1809. A Bible record of one of his grandsons gives names and dates of birth of 12 children, 10 of whom (5 boys, 5 girls) survived infancy. Two of the boys, Joshua and Isaac, remained in Estill County to become substantial citizens. William went to Logan County, KY where some of his descendants still live. David went to Logan County,

KY, then to Pike County, IL where he died in 1831; four of his sons and a daughter migrated to Texas before the Civil War, where they have numerous descendants. The youngest son John went to Simpson or Logan County, KY, then to Illinois, and spent the last 20 years of his life in Lawrence County, in southwestern Missouri; he died in Kansas City, MO in 1864. A daughter, Martha, married Eli Briant and lived in Logan County, KY. We have not been able to make contact with descendants of the other four" (Miller Jr., 1985).

Sidney Barnes Connection

"Sidney Madison Barnes, husband of Elizabeth Mize, daughter of Isaac and Elizabeth Mize, is arguably the most notable individual ever born within the boundaries of Estill County. He possessed many of the same attributes of Green Clay, in that he too was a soldier, politician and an entrepreneur. He was the county's most influential citizen during the critical period prior to and during the Civil War. He, like Clay, left his imprint on the Estill County as well.

Sidney was born in 1821 to John Harris Barnes and Lucy Grubbs. John and Lucy Barnes, while still in their twenties, died when one of the frequent Typhoid Fever epidemics struck Irvine in 1823/24. At the death of their parents, Sidney and his younger brother Thomas Barnes were sent to live with an uncle in Montgomery County.

Thomas Grubbs was a farmer and insisted that his eldest nephew become a farmer. However, Sidney was interested in following his father into the legal profession. When he reached the age of eighteen he rebelled against his uncle and returned to Irvine to pursue a career in law. According to granddaughter, Maude Barnes Miller, Sidney's net assets when he arrived in his native county were a horse, a dollar and a watch.

Sidney did odd jobs around the courthouse while his father's old friend, Judge Burnham, tutored him in law. After completing his legal training, he became one of Estill County's most successful attorneys for the next three decades. In 1841, Sidney married Elizabeth Mize, daughter of Isaac and Elizabeth Mize.

Isaac Mize was a wealthy landowner whose holdings included the well-known spa, Estill Springs. Sidney and Elizabeth had six children, several of whom became prominent in their own right. Their eldest son, Thomas Harris Barnes, left Centre College after the outbreak of the Civil War to become one of the youngest persons ever promoted to the rank of Major in the U S Army.

In later life he was appointed Prosecuting Attorney for the Western District of Arkansas by President McKinley.

Another son, James Keith Barnes served as postmaster of Fort Smith, Arkansas. The house that James Keith Barnes constructed while living in Fort Smith has recently been given museum status by the Arkansas Heritage Commission. When the Civil War erupted, Sidney rallied to the side of the Union. He was the prime force in the formation of the famous Eighth Kentucky Infantry Regiment. The regiment was comprised mostly of men from Estill and her neighboring counties. The soldiers earned national acclaim for their heroic efforts in capturing the crest of Lookout Mountain in that celebrated battle. The names of Sidney and several of his subordinates are enshrined on a plaque atop the precipice.

Sidney's plantation at Estill Springs became the training base for the Eighth Infantry while the regiment was being assembled. Sidney had acquired the estate from his father-in-law just prior to the outbreak of the Civil War. Barnes was given a Colonel's commission and assumed command of the regiment. As commanding officer, he is credited for much of the success achieved by the unit" (Chazzcreations, 2015).

Mize, Boone, Lincoln connection

"It was in the Yadkin Valley in western North Carolina that our forefather, Joshua Mize, lived during the year 1784. Yadkin Valley is located in present Wilkes County, North Carolina, near the eastern face of the Blue Ridge Mountains. It was in this remote area that the family of Joshua and his wife Patty lived.

This was approximately 30 miles from the Boone Family settlement. Squire Boone, the father of Daniel Boone bought land close to Holman's Ford located on the North Fork of the Yadkin Valley in present day Davidson County, North Carolina. Squire had traveled from Berks County, Pennsylvania between the years 1751 and 1752 to North Carolina.

The Boone family had married several times into the John Lincoln family of Berk's County, Pennsylvania. John Lincoln's grandson, Abraham Lincoln (grandfather of the President Abraham Lincoln), moved through Virginia into Kentucky, through Cumberland

Gap via the Wilderness Trail. Because of this, our Mize family can claim being related to President Abraham Lincoln albeit only distantly.

Squire Boone fathered several children but there are three sons which are pertinent to the Boone/Mize connection. They were Samuel, George, and Daniel. Daniel married Rebecca Bryan, whose family was a neighbor to the Boones, during the year 1756. During the year 1759 he bought 640 acres from his father George Boone to live on. Just five years later, he sold this land and moved farther up the Yadkin Valley located in Wilkes County, North Carolina in 1769.

During the same time frame, there was major discontent between the British government and the colonial settlers. A vigilante group named the Regulators regularly fought the British government troops and the government because of their oppressive policies. Violence was a common occurrence filtering through the valley during the Revolution War.

Back to 1769, Daniel Boone was recruited as a scout for an expedition through the Cumberland Gap and up into the region where the Kentucky River and the Licking River are located. This expedition established a base at the adjunct of present-day Estill, Powell and Clark counties on the Red River. It was during this expedition, that Boone visited a buffalo wallow near the Red River which was named Estill Springs which is close to the present-day town of Irvine.

Irvine is where the Isaac Mize family settled. Daniel helped to establish the Wilderness Road during the year 1774 and he ultimately established Fort Boonesboro in late 1775. He brought his family from the Yadkin Valley in North Carolina to Fort Boonesboro settlement on the banks of the Kentucky River. Daniel had several children but of specific importance were Elizabeth, William L. and Squire.

Nancy Grubbs, married William L. Boone on 16 August 1789 in Madison County, Kentucky. Remember Lucy Grubbs? Well she married John Barnes and they had a son named Sidney M. Barnes. Sidney Barnes was a very respected lawyer of Estill County, Kentucky and became very involved in politics.

He bought four hundred acres of land at Estill Springs located in Estill County' Kentucky along with enough slaves to farm the land and attend his family. He was a southerner at heart but ultimately held the

Union cause during the Civil War. He became the Colonel of the 8th Kentucky Volunteer Infantry which he raised and trained on his land at Estill Springs.

After the Civil War, he served as a Representative in the Kentucky House of Representatives during 1848 and later ran for Governor during 1867 which he subsequently lost the election. He then moved to Arkansas where he became a delegate in the 1874 Constitutional Convention. He was nominated and appointed as the U.S. District Attorney for the Territory of New Mexico.

Sidney and his wife spent their last days in Carthage, Missouri. Joshua Mize, who had lived in North Carolina, fathered a son, Isaac, which married an Elizabeth. That union between Isaac (Sr.) and Elizabeth produced a son named Isaac (Jr.) who married Nancy Walker. The marriage between Isaac and Nancy produced a daughter named Elizabeth.

So far, so good. Remember Sidney Barnes? Sidney married Elizabeth, the daughter of Isaac (Jr.) Mize and Nancy Walker. This is the connection from the Mize family to the Grubbs family which in turn connects to Boone family.

Long story short.... The Boones married into the Grubbs family. Sidney M. Barnes, the son of Lucy Grubbs and John Barnes, married Elizabeth Mize, the daughter of Isaac Mize and Nancy Walker! We are related but only distantly to Boone Family and still even more distantly to the Lincoln Family" (Chazzcreations, 2015).

New Research

"According to the Church of Latter-Day Saints' family history website for worldwide sources, there were Mize's living in England as far back as the 1500s in Lancashire County, near Manchester. The earliest reference is to the marriage of Thomas Mize to Margaret Buernsell in Manchester Cathedral December 12th, 1595" (Chazzcreations, 2015).

"Ruth Mize B: 02/09/1808 VA. D: 10/09/1878 Mercer Cty, WV. M: 03/17/1825 to Henry Clark, son of Jesse Clark and Lucy Jane Pedigo. B: 1806 Va. D: 1882 WV. They had 10 children..." (Chazzcreations, 2015).

"She was married to Henry Clark (son of Jesse Clark and Lucy Jane Pedigo) 17 Mar 1825 on Thursday in Patrick Co. VA. **Henry Clark** was born about 1806 in Patrick Co. VA. He died about 1882 in Mercer Co. WV. He was buried. We have not been able to find when

Henry died. Bob DID fine the graves of Henry and Ruth in their family cemetery in Camp Creek. It is called the Clark Cemetery. They have home-made markers and are side by side. Henry lived with John until he died sometime after 1880. John is also buried there" (Angelfire, 2015).

"Henry and Ruth ran the Clark's Inn at Camp Creek in the 1800's. Henry seems to have been a man who was always ready to make a dime, and was quite good at it. There was a famous Civil War battle fought at the home of Henry and Ruth and is written in books that can be found in the local Library's.

Ruth refused to leave her home when the North came and took over her house. She stayed inside with some of her small children and the Northern Troops. The next morning a battle was fought between Cox's Army and the Flat Top Copperheads, captained by the famous Richard Foley.

One can only guess at what Ruth had to say to the Union Troop's. She had to be a very brave lady to stay and face the Union Troop's without Henry there to back her up. I am sure that they were more than happy to depart her home the next morning, and the fight with Richard Foley and his Copperheads had to be mild to what she had put them through.

She is a lady to be admired by all of her descendants, men and women. She is also a good example for our young girls today. I can't help but wonder how many of us would be as brave? I have also wondered where Henry was, that Ruth was in the home alone except for her small children? Could he have gone into the nearby mountains to warn Capt. Richard Foley? It is very likely that he did and was unable to get back, or he could have fought with the Copperheads.

When the State of West Virginia tore down and burned the Clark home to make a new road, Josiah Carl Clark says there were balls still in bedded it the logs from the battle fought there in 1862. It would have been nice if the State could or would have saved the home as a Historical building. Maybe too, I only wish for this because they were my great-great grandparents.

Henry and Ruth came to this area in 1842 according to their son, Henry, Jr. They first bought property in Wyoming Co. Virginia, then sometime before 1860 they sold that to a William Clark (don't know what relation, but am sure there is one) and bought the property in Camp Creek where they lived out their lives. Henry gave the property to their son John and lived there with him until he died sometime before 1890" (Chazzcreations, 2015).

"**Issac Mize** born 1755 in Wilkes Cty. NC D: Oct 1809. He was buried in Estill County, KY. M:2) 1775 Elizabeth (Massay?) in Surry County, NC B: D: 1813. Isaac was a farmer in Estill Cty, adjoining Estill Springs at Irvine, which he owned at one time. Isaac was in the KY Legislature 1830, 1831, and 1839. He was a Sheriff in 1836 and a Judge. Most of the family supported the Confederacy except for daughter Elizabeth. They had at least 8 children:

1-Rebeeca Mize B: 07/09/1776   D: 05/02/1814   M: 07/24/1794 John Moore

2~Nancy Mize B: 02/12/1778 D: 04/02/1780

3~William M. Mize B: 01/07/1780 D: 07/04/1824 M: 12/22/1803 Lucy Proctor

1~John Proctor Mize B: 08/28/1805 KY D: 06/03/1887 KY M: Nancy M. Linton B: 1809 D: 1840 M: 2) Comfort Richardson B: 1818 D: 1848 M: 3) Elizabeth Ginter

1~Lucy Ellen Mize B: 1840 D: 1889

2~Sara Mize B: 1807 D: 1822

3~Elizabeth Mize B: 1809 D: 1836

4~Nancy Mize B: 1811 D: M: Robert E. Collins

5~Isaac Mize B: 1815 D:

4~Joshua Mize B: 02/03/1782 D: 03/14/1852 M: 08/01/1803 Elizabeth Betsy Witt B: 1783 VA D: 1852

1~Milton Mize B: 1804

2~Elizabeth Mize B: 12/29/1807 D: 12/03/1878 M: 10/15/1826 John H. Riddell B: 01/23/1808 D: 10/13/1864

1~Robert Riddell B: 1833 D: 02/11/1938 M: 1857 Ann Maria Tobey

3~Mary Mize   B: 1810 D: M: Presley Harris

4~Nancy Mize   B: 1812 D: 1899 M: Johnson Pigg

5~William Mize B: 1814 D: 1890 M: Caroline Hoyt Jacobs

6~Martin Mize   B: 1816 D:

7~Lucy Mize   B: 1820 D: 1890 M: John Nelson M: 2) James McKinney

8~Hal Mize   B: 1821 D:

5~Ann Mize B: 09/17/1783 D:

6~David Mize B: 10/15/1785 KY D: 07/04/1837 IL M: 11/26/1806 Hannah Peter B: 08/26/1789 KY D: 01/29/1831 IL

1~Lila Dorinda Gaither Mize B: 02/28/1808 KY D: 10/30/1880 TX M: 05/06/1824 John Neeley B: 04/10/1803 TN D: 09/21/1879 TX

2~Martha Hogg Mize   B: 10/13/1809 KY D: 1842 IL M: 11/22/1832 IL Benjamin Evans Dunnaway B: 1802 KY D: 10/1856 OR

3~Samuel Peter Mize B: 10/12/1811 KY D: 04/06/1879 TX M: 06/29/1834 Jemimah Hendrick B: D: 03/08/1837 IL

4~Isaac Ike Mize B: 03/14/1814 KY D: MO M: Martha Snow B: Ky D: MO

5~Simon Peter Mize B: 03/10/1816 KY D: 1900

6~John Mize B: 09/14/1818 KY D: M: 08/04/1842 Lucy Melvina Chamberling B: D:

7~Mary Mize B: 12/28/1820 D: M: 1852 John Stanburg Stanborky

8~David Mize B: 08/26/1823 KY D: 09/28/1848 TX M: 1842 Sally Ann Weir

9~Zachariah P. Mize B: 09/30/1825 IL D: 1880 TX M: Delilah A. Ingram IL. B: 1830 D: 1918

10~James M. Mize B: 02/14/1828 IL D: 1865 TX M: Sophonia A. (or Sophronia G.) Heflin B: 1841apx D: 1914apx TX

11~ElizabethMize B: 05/15/1830 IL D: 09/26/1830 IL

7~Elizabeth Mize B: 12/26/1787 D: M: 1815 Robert Elerson Estill Cty, KY

8~Mary Mize B: 09/23/1789 D:

9~Martha Patsy Mize B: 09/30/1791 KY D: 01/27/1875 KY M: 12/18/1815 Eli Briant B: 03/08/1789 NC D: 11/01/1864 KY

Isaac Mize Jr. B: 11/26/1792 D: 3/26/1882 in Estill Cty, KY. Isaac Mize was one of the leading citizens of his community in Estill County, where he was engaged in farming and stock trading, and served in the State Legislature and Judge. He married on 03/14/1819 to Nancy Walker in Estill County, KY. She was born 07/28/1798 at the mouth of Red Lick Creek in Estill County, KY and died 03/13/1860 in Estill County, KY and is buried at Irvine City Cemetary.

Nancy had a wealthy brother, James Morgan Walker. It has been said that the first fighting in the Civil War, War Between the States, was on his farm in Boone Cty., Missouri. A grandson, Thomas J. Walker, had The Virginia Pharmacy in Independence, MO (father of Henrietta Walker Childers of Independence).

Nancy Walker's sister, Betsy married Thomas Gaddy in Estill Cty in 1815. They went to Illinois about 1833. The Walker family probably came from Northern Ireland, though somesay Alsasce-Lorraine. They had eight children:

1~**John Aleis Mize** B: 01/17/1820 in Estill County, KY D: 12/21/1847 Irvine, where he had been engaged in merchandising. **See Family History:**

2~Elizabeth Mize B: 1822 in Estill Co., KY. D: 1904 M: 1841 Sidney Madison Barnes, son of John Harris Barnes and Lucy Grubbs B: 1821 D: 1890 MO. Union Army: Eighth Kentucky Infantry Regiment. 6 children. See additional information below.

3~Nancy Mize was born in 1824 in Estill Co., KY. D: 1891 M: 1846 James Greenville Trimble B: 1823 D: 1919 **See Trimble History**

4~Roderick Shackleford Mize B: 1827 Estill Cty, KY. D: 1868 at Independence. Missouri, where he was formerly a proprietor of the old ferry, and where his descendants still live M: Katherine Daniel B: 1834 D: 1894

5~Susan J. Mize B: 1829 D: 1898 M: George W. Lyle B: 1839   D: 1910 M:2) George Maple M:3) Phillip Claiborn Eubank B: 1809 D: 1880 in Millers Creek, Estill, KY

    1~Roderick M. Eubank:

    2~Simpson Grant Eubank lived in Howard Cty., Missouri, where he died in 1906, near Armstrong. M: Lizzie Lee 5 children:

        1~Vallnon Eubank   B: D: M: now in Texas

        2~Philip Lee Eubank B: D: M:

3~Reuben Mize Eubank   B: D: M:

4~Floyd Richard Eubank B: D: M:

5~Bruce Eubank   B: D: M:

6~Robert Mize B: 1832 Estill Cty, KY D: 1855

7~'Daughter' Mize was born in 1834 in Estill Co., KY.

8~Frances C. Mize B: 1836 in Estill Cty, KY. D: 1917 M: 1865 William Birchie Benton B: 1833 D: 1908

9~Issac Mize III B: 1840 D: 1898 M: 08/25/1857 Edith M. Vaughn B: 08/31/1841 KY D: 10/20/1910 Estill Cty, after a career in farming. 9 children:

1~James Greene Mize B: 1858 Estill Cty KY eldest son, was a leading merchant of Vaughn's Mill in Powell County D: 1895 M: Dolly Coleman Littlepage.

2~Florence Mize B: 1860 D: 1946 M: 1879 James Marshall Locknane

3~Samuel B: 1862 D: 1891 M: Susan Mahill Samuel was a farmer in Estill County

4~Roderick Mize B: 1865 in Estill Co., KY. D: 1889

5~Nancy/Nannie Mize B: 1867 in Estill Co., KY. D: 1949 M: 1885 JW John William McKinney B: 1856 D: 1919

6~John William Mize B: 1868 in Estill Co., KY. D: 1947 M: 1889 Lena Rivers Wright B: 1874 D: 1947 Resident of Vaughn's Mill.

7~Mattie Bush Mize B: 1872 in Estill Co., KY. D: 1942 M: Walter Raleigh Day B: 1873 D: 1937

8~Auguston S. Mize B: 1874 in Estill Co., KY. D: 1901 M: Lou Ann McKinney

9~William Olden Mize B: 1877 in Estill Co., KY. D: 1965 M: Ouida Weeda Tipton M: 2) Harriet McKnight

10~Minnie Margie Mize B: 1880 in Estill Co., KY. D: 1912 M: Abraham Roger Hale

11~Robert Mize B: 1882 D:

12~Katherine Mize B: 1884 D: M: Isa Haggard M: 2) William Hickman

Isaac's daughter married Col. Sidney M. Barnes, a colonel of the Federal Army during the War Between the States, and former proprietor of Eubank Springs, who died at Little Rock

11~John Mize B: 11/28/1796 D: 08/21/1797

12~John Mize B: 03/18/1799 KY D: 09/09/1864 MO M: 1823 Mary Ann Snow B: 06/29/1807 KY D: 02/09/1871 MO

9~Edie (Edey) Mize was born 1756 M: Taylor Chambers?

10~Nancy Mize was born 1757 M: ~Brown" (Chazzcreations, 2015).

"William Oldham Mize, a son of John A. Mize, married Luella Cockrell and was a merchant at Hazel Green, where he died, and enrolling clerk in the House of Representatives for several terms.

He was a fine Christian gentleman and passed away at the age of sixty-five years at Hazel Green, where his son, Carl, lived. J. Greene Mize, the eldest son in the large family of Isaac Mize, the younger, was a leading merchant of Vaughn's Mill, Powell County. Another son, Samuel, was also a farmer in Estill County, and married Susan Mahill, and a third son, John W., was a resident of Vaughn's Mill" (Chazzcreations, 2015).

Descendants of Benjamin Mize and Rachel Richardson

"Researching Benjamin's family has been difficult because of the numerous shifts and creation of counties in Virginia during the mid and late 1700's.

Some have speculated that Benjamin Mize was born about 1755 in Lunenburg Co., Virginia in the area that was to be later part of Henry Co., Virginia. However, since his father, Joshua Mize moved to Anson Co., North Carolina about 1752 he was probably was born in what was originally part of Anson County.

The next year, in 1753, this same area was taken to form Rowan County. In 1771 Surry County, and lastly in 1777 was made part of Wilkes County.

The first public record I have found of Benjamin Mize comes from the book Surry & Wilkes Co., North Carolina Taxables 1771-1800. The 1774 Surry County Taxables lists him and his father, Joshua Mize.

Apparently, Benjamin moved from Surry Co., North Carolina

Patrick Co., VA., by 1775 as his father is only found in the 1775 Surry County Taxables. Evidence that supports this is that all Census Records of his children list themselves as born in Virginia as well as grandchildren listing their parents as born in Virginia.

Soon after his Joshua Mize's death in 1790, we find Benjamin selling lands in Patrick Co., Virginia.

Patrick Co., Virginia Land Records: 24, Apr. 1804, David Crews purchased 246 acres on South branch of Smith River from Benjamin Mize for 500 pounds. Deed Bk. 2: page 330

12 Sept. 1804 David Crews and Thomas Craddock to Benjamin Mize sold one tract of land containing 80 acres more or less lying and being in Patrick Co. on Gobling Town Creek. Witnessed: James Cradock, Moses Waldorn, Jacob Blackburn & James Mize

Recorded: April 1805 Barron Co., Kentucky.

Benjamin is found in the 1800 Rowan Co., North Carolina Federal Census, pg. 410 which lists Benjamin Mize 1 male under 10, 1 male 26-45, 1 female under 10, 1 female 16-26.

The above deed proves that Benjamin Mize and his son James Mize were in Barren Co., Kentucky at least by 1804. This is the migration pattern of Benjamin's children as evidenced by their children's place of birth as listed in various census records and land deeds.

John Mize, Born about 1775, Patrick Co., Virginia. Having been married in 1800, he was well established in home at the time of the move and therefore didn't take part in the migration.

James Mize Born about 1777, Patrick Co., Virginia. Moved to Barren Co., Kentucky by 1805, resided there until at least 1823.Moved to Fountain Co., Indiana by 1829 where he died June 05, 1831.

Issac Mize Born about 1785, Patrick Co., Virginia, was in Tennessee 1811-1812, in Barren Co., Kentucky by 1814.Resided there until his death before 1850.He and wife, Ruth were divorced in 1838 in Barren Co., Kentucky and soon afterwards she moved to Shelby Co., Illinois where she died about 1855.

David Mize Born about 1790, Patrick Co., Virginia, was in Barren Co., Kentucky by 1812.He lived in the NE part of the county near the border of Metcalfe Co., Kentucky. Died between 1850-1853 as evidenced by probate of his lands" (therock6250, 2010).

Much more information about different branches of the Mize family, as well as some pictures can be found on the Internet at http://www.genealogy.com/ftm/h/a/r/James-C-Harmon/index.html

My Lineage

The point of this project was to trace my direct lineage on my mother's side of my family from myself back to Isaac Mize, and further if possible. It is here that I will attempt to show my direct lineage, and where-ever it is possible I will also add the reference number of the person from 'the Isaac Mize Family of Eastern Kentucky' by Franklin Miller Jr. This same type of lineage tracing can be done by every branch of the Isaac Mize family.

1.) I will start my lineage trace by starting with myself, Gerald C. Jones M9993231. From there the line goes back through my mother Joan Williams M999323.

2.) Joan Williams M999323. From there the lineage goes through her mother Blanche Williams.

3.) Blanche Williams M99932. From there it goes back through her mother Katherine Forest Mize M9993.

4.) Katherine Forest Mize M9993. From there the lineage goes back through her father William Olden Mize M999.

5.) William Olden Mize M999. From there it goes back through his father Isaac Mize M99.

6.) Isaac Mize M99. I remember reading somewhere that it was this Isaac Mize that was referred to as Jr., and in another reading, I seen he was referred to as Isaac Mize III. However, neither version has been proven yet. From here the lineage goes back through Isaac Mize M9.

7.) Isaac Mize M9. It is this Isaac Mize that I believe to be the Isaac Mize that was married to Nancy Walker, and also served in the Kentucky Legislature in 1830, 1831, and in 1839. From here the lineage goes back through his father Isaac Mize, the origination of the number system used by Franklin Miller Jr.

8.) Isaac Mize (M). This is the Isaac Mize that is referred to in the book titled 'The Isaac Mize Family of Eastern Kentucky'. He was born in 1752 and died in 1809, and in one reference he was listed as having a middle name of Keziah. This is where most of the facts about our genealogy stop. However, as you have probably already gathered by the stories you have already read, that there are traces of a further lineage. From here I believe the lineage goes back through Isaac's father to Joshua Mize (1727 – 1790).

9.) Joshua Mize (1727 – 1790). Little can be found about this man at the moment, but we are always looking for new information. From here the lineage goes back through his father to Jeremiah Mize (1694 – 1775).

10.) Jeremiah Mize (1694 – 1775). It is believed that this man was referred to as Jeremiah Mize Sr. at one point in time. There is also little information available about this man as well. From here the lineage goes back through his father to James Mize.

11.) James Mize. It is this James Mize that I believe was shown as being taxed in Virginia in 1694-1698. It is at this time that I must remind you that people were only taxed once they became older than 15 or 16 years of age. So, this date for him is not a birth date. I have also seen reference to this man being referred to as James Mize II. From here the lineage goes back through his father to James Mize I.

12.) James Mize I. all that is shown at this time for James Mize I is a birth date of 1645 in Manchester England. From here it is believed that the lineage goes back through his father to Thomas Mize.

13.) Thomas Mize. All that is known about this man at the moment is a record from The Church of Latter-Day Saints in England that list a marriage in 1595.

Please keep in mind that this may not be perfect in its accuracy. Some of the dates could be wrong, since I do remember seeing conflicts with the dates from one reference to another. Therefore, mistakes could be shown, and will be corrected as soon as they are known to this author. Steps 9-13 are the sections that I am referring to at this time.

I would also like to add an addition to this personal genealogical story, and that is a newly learned connection to the Daniel Boone family. The connection is through one of my younger sisters' husband, J. Galloway. He is a direct descendant of Daniel Boone himself, and as such adds a direct personal relationship to the Daniel Boone Family. Thank you, J. Galloway, for being a good husband to one of my little sisters, and father to your children.

ISAAC MIZE FAMILY

Summary

"Isaac Mize and wife Elizabeth had 12 children. Two of the children died in infancy. The 10 surviving children are given code numbers Ml, M2, ... through MA.

The only daughter whose descendants are known is Martha Mize Briant, so this summary is not a complete list. It is the best we can do.

Ml. Rebecca Mize (1776-1814) m. John Moore probably lived in Logan County, KY

 — Nancy Mize (1778-1990) (Infant)

M2. William Mize (1780-1824) Lived in Logan County, KY

 m. Lucy Proctor

 M21.John Proctor Mize (1805-1887)

  m(l). Nancy M. Linton — 1 dau.

  m(2).Comfort Richardson — 4 ch.

m(3).Elizabeth O'Roark — 3 ch.

M22.Sarah Mize (1807-1822)

M23.Elizabeth Mize (1809-1836)

M24.Nancy Mize (1811)

m. Robert E. Collins — 4 ch.

M25.Isaac Mize (1815)

M3. Joshua Mize (1782-1852) Lived in Estill County, KY

m. Elizabeth Witt

M31.Milton G. Mize (1804?)

M32.Elizabeth Mize (1807-1878)

m. John H. Riddell — 10 ch.

M33. Mary Mize (1810?)

m. Presley Harris — 5 ch. Went to Missouri

M34.Nancy Mize (1812-1899)

m. Johnson Pigg — 9 ch.

M35.William Mize (1814-1890)

m. Caroline Hoyt Jacobs — 5 ch.

M36. Martin Mize (1816?)

M37.Lucy Mize (1820-1890)

m(1). John Nelson Smith — 9 ch.

m(2). James McKinney

M38. Hal Mize (1821?)

M4. Ann Mize (1783)

M5. David Mize (1785-1831) Went to Pike County, IL

m. Hannah Peter

M51. (Lila) Dorinda Gaither Mize (1808-1880) Went to Texas

m. John Neeley — 11 ch.

M52.Martha Hogg Mize (1809 - ca 1842)

m. Benjamin Evans Dunaway — 5 ch.

M53.Samuel Peter Mize (1811-1879) Went to Texas

m(1). Jemima Hendrick — 2 ch.

m(2).Beersheba Dodson — 13 ch

M54.Isaac Mize (1814) Went to Lawrence County, MO

m. Martha at least 5 ch.

M55.Simon Mize (1816)

m. Sarah F. Dunaway

M56.John Mize (1818)

M57.Mary Mize

m. Stanburg

M58.David Mize (1823-1848) Went to Texas

m. Sally Ann Weir — 2 ch.

M59. Zachariah Mize (1825-ca 1880) Went to Texas

m. Delilah A. Ingram — 7 ch.

M5A.James M. Mize (1828-1864) Went to Texas

m. Sophronia G. Heflin — 1 dau.

M5B.Elizabeth Mize (b. and d. 1830)

M6. Elizabeth Mize (1787)

m. Robert Elerson

M8. Martha Mize (1791-1875) Lived in Logan County, KY

m. Eli Briant — 11 ch. Names of only 7 are known

M81.Edward Briant (1818-1865)

m. Matilda Jane Stewart — 12 ch.

M82.Mary Briant (Polly) (1819-1878)

m. William P. Cushenberry — 9 ch.

M86. Presley Briant (?) (no further information)

M87.William Briant (1826-1888)

m. Sarah Frances Swearingen — 8 ch.

M89.Rebecca J. Briant (1829-1892)

m(l). John W. Ennis — 3 ch.

m(2).Joseph Venable — 6 ch., plus 5 stepchildren

M8A.Martha Jane Briant (1830-1881)

m. William Ezra Harris — 6 ch.

M8B.Malinda Briant (Lin) (1833-1906)

m. Leonard R. Arnold (Lem) — no ch.

M9. Isaac Mize (1792-1882) Lived in Estill County, KY

m. Nancy Walker

M91.John A. Mize (1820-1847) Went to Missouri

m. Marium Oldham — 1 son

M92.Elizabeth Mize (1822-1904)

m. Sidney Madison Barnes — 6 ch.

M93.Nancy Mize (1824-1891)

m. (James) Greenville Trimble — 9 ch.

M94.Roderick Shackleford Mize (1827-1868) Went to Missouri

m. Katharine Daniel — 6 ch.

M95.Susan J. Mize (1829-1898)

m(1). George Mapel — 3 ch.

m(2).Philip Claiborne Eubank — 2 sons

m(3).George W. Lyle — 1 son

M96.Robert Mize (ca 1833 - ca 1854) Went to Missouri

M97. Mize (ca 1835) A daughter, died young

M98.Fannie C. Mize (ca 1837 - 1917)

m. (William) Birchie Benton — 6 ch.

M99.Isaac Mize, Jr. (1840-1898)

m. Edith M. Vaughn — 12 ch.

— John Mize (1796-1797) (Infant)

MA. John Mize (1799-1864) Lived in KY, IL, and went to Lawrence County, MO

    m. Mary Ann Snow

    MAI. Martha Mize (ca 1824-1842) d. in IL. unm.

    MA2.Elizabeth Margaret Mize (ca 1826-1870)

        m. Alexander J. T. Mahan — 1 son

    MA3.Julia Ann Mize (1828-1892)

        m. William A. Downey — 4 ch.

    MA4.Louisa Mize (Eliza) (ca 1835)

        m. Robinson Starrett — at least 5 ch.

    MA5.Martin Mize (1836-1905)

        m(1). Rebecca Snow — 7 ch.

    MA6.John F. Mize (1838-1910)

        m. Delilah — 3 sons

    MA7.Jesse Mize (ca 1840)

        m. — 3 ch.

    MA8.William Hamilton Mize (ca 1845-1907)

        m. Julia Frances Spilman — 3 ch.

MA9.James Mize (1853-1933)

m. Lucy Robertson — 4 ch." (Miller Jr., 1984).

If you will notice, there is one small error in this quote. It is in M1 where it shows Nancy Mize (1778-1990). Obviously, she did not live that long, and if she did she needs to share her secret with the rest of us. There is also not a M7 listed in the list.

References

Angelfire, (2015), *Descendants of James Mize, Sr.* Retrieved from,

http://www.angelfire.com/va2/rineharts/mize.htm

Chazzcreations, (2015), *Mize~Oldham~Swope~Cockrell.* Retrieved

from, http://www.chazzcreations.com/mize_genealogy

Miller Jr., F., (1985), *The Isaac Mize Family of Eastern Kentucky.*

Retrievedfrom,https://dcms.lds.org/delivery/DeliveryManagerSe

rvlet?dps_pid=IE923910

therock6250, (2015), *Descendants of Benjamin Mize and Rachel

Richardson.*,Retrievedfrom,http://www.genealogy.com/ftm/h/a/r

/James-C-Harmon/index.html